THE ELEPHANT IN THE YOUTH ROOM

Pastoral Care for Teens

by Jim Chesnes & Kevin Driscoll

The information contained herein is published and produced by Life Teen, Inc. The resources and practices are in full accordance with the Roman Catholic Church. The Life Teen® name and associated logos are trademarks registered with the United States Patent and Trademark Office. Use of the Life Teen® trademarks without prior permission is forbidden. Permission may be requested by contacting Life Teen, Inc. at 480-820-7001.

Cover design by Carlos Weaver

ISBN: 978-0-9802362-2-4

Copyright ©2011 Life Teen, Inc. All rights reserved.

Published by Life Teen, Inc.
2222 S. Dobson Rd.
Suite 601
Mesa, AZ 85202
www.lifeteen.com

Printed in the United States of America.
Printed on acid-free paper.

For more information about Life Teen or to order additional copies, go online to www.lifeteen.com or call us at 1-800-809-3902.

Dedication

This book is dedicated to
Our parents Jerry, Rosemarie, Vince, and Marie
- our first youth ministers.
Our wives, Laura and Lisa
- master teachers and full time Saints.
Our kids, Mary, Max, Brett and J. P.
- our future Church.

Table of Contents

Introduction

THE ELEPHANT IN
THE YOUTH ROOM

The apex of salvation history is upon us: we gather as a community of believers around our priest *in persona Christi* as he lifts the host for consecration, reminding us of Christ's ultimate sacrifice and our salvation. Just then you hear an inappropriate sound and a chuckle from a few rows back. You already know who it is.

After Mass, you approach the young man about his behavior and he apologizes. Again. He has done this type of thing before. You have heard comments from parishioners who are "offended by the teen's behavior at Mass," but you believe something more is going on. Other young people his age either ignore him or make fun of him. Younger kids think he is hilarious, so he gravitates towards them. The priest wants to speak with you.

When you were hired as a youth minister (or appointed, or left the pastor little choice when you begged for the opportunity to wear three dozen free t-shirts), you accepted a laundry list of unwritten job descriptions. One is to be an advocate for youth, believing in their potential, and "getting their back," especially to those in your church or community who don't always think too highly of God's young Church.

Usually it's easy: put up a few pictures of them painting houses for senior citizens, or have a well-groomed one stand up and read a passage from Thessalonians once in a while (They'll be impressed that she can even pronounce 'Thessalonians!'). But now you have to stand behind *him*, the one that gives you fits at night. The one making life miserable for everyone around him, and the one hurting your ability to minister to the other "good" kids.

When done well, youth ministry is attractive to hurting kids. We are called to be people who love the unlovable. An adolescent dealing with problems can be very unlovable. Trite though the lesson may be, the Bible reminds us to love thy neighbor...even if that neighbor makes every youth ministry gathering an adventure.

How do we minister to kids who are obviously dealing with problems? How do we know exactly what we are looking at when we see a kid act out? How do we minister to the individual without compromising our ministry to the rest? What do we do with "the elephant in the youth room?"

What follows is a discussion about some of the common problems of adolescence, and how youth ministers can work with these very special children of God.

We will first meet the adolescent brain, a complex and changing place. Then we will look at some of the emotional problems commonly faced by teens: moods, behaviors, and attention problems. We'll explore the many communities in which teens live, in the flesh and online. We will address ministry with special needs youth, substance abuse and addictions, and how to respond to a crisis. You will be equipped with a basic understanding of the minds and behaviors of the "elephants" you are called to serve, and strategies for how to best bring the light of Christ into darkness. We'll also pause to reflect on our own needs, because we know how common it can be to devote our entire everything into helping teens, then forget that we have our own needs.

Who "we" are

The "we" you'll read about throughout this book are two servants of God not unlike yourself. Jim Chesnes and Kevin Driscoll met in 1999, when Kevin was hired as the associate director of youth ministry for the Diocese of Palm Beach, Florida. Jim was (and, God willing, still is) the youth ministry coordinator for one of the parishes in the diocese, St. Paul of the Cross Catholic Church in North Palm Beach. A friendship was forged quickly as they waited in dozens of gelato shops across Italy on their pilgrimage to Rome for World Youth Day 2000.

Early in Jim's ministry career he became educated and licensed in mental health counseling. His emphasis on youth and family matters has long been an asset to his ministry. In addition to the many hats he wears for his parish, he maintains a private practice as well.

In the early part of the 2000s, youth ministers throughout the diocese would gather regularly for fellowship, breaking bread and "talking shop." On more than a few occasions, youth ministers, knowing of Jim's qualifications, would present to Jim the many pastoral situations that left them confused, baffled, or frustrated.

Kevin believed then—as he does now—that of all the ministry components of *Renewing the Vision: A Framework for Catholic Youth Ministry*, the USCCB document on Catholic youth ministry, the Ministry of Pastoral Care speaks most accurately to the secular world in which teens live. Unfortunately, when teens are in need of help, and when youth ministers seek resources to provide that help, there are few resources available.

Kevin and his family relocated to Northwest Indiana in 2003 when Kevin became the director of youth ministry in the Diocese of Gary, Indiana. Driven by a desire to minister to the ministers, he took to the roads of his diocese ready to help build better youth ministry. He found teens— and youth ministers—facing the same "ick" he saw in south Florida, and once again found himself turning to Jim for his professional insights.

We all agree there are teens everywhere in need of pastoral care. But how do we provide it? For not only the teens, but also ourselves?

In 2005, Jim and Kevin first spoke on this topic when they presented a workshop at the National Catholic Youth Conference that fall in Atlanta. On the heels of Hurricane Katrina, the workshop was designed to assist youth ministers looking to provide a crisis response. Not only did they meet youth ministers from communities destroyed by storms, they also met youth ministers from communities destroyed by suicide, car accidents, drug abuse, divorce, cults, the list goes on.

The two have continued to speak nationally about the Ministry of Pastoral Care within the context of Catholic Youth Ministry. Each brings a unique perspective to the topic: Jim holds a bachelor of arts in philosophy/religion from Flagler College in St. Augustine, FL and a master of science in mental health counseling from Nova Southeastern University in Fort Lauderdale, FL. Kevin owns a bachelor of science in mass communications/broadcasting from Illinois State University in Normal, IL and a master of arts in pastoral studies from Catholic Theological Union in Chicago, IL.

Together the two have teamed up to share one real passion in youth ministry: a burning desire to reach out and help youth ministers help teens in need of Christ's healing presence. The "we" you'll read throughout this book is not only for grammatical consistency! It is a ministry WE take seriously, humbly led by a desire to serve Christ.

Where humility and competency meet

We've heard this a lot: "I'm not qualified to provide professional assistance. I'm not a counselor." We appreciate that, and in fact that was the inspiration for writing this book. Too often we see youth ministers avoid problems altogether, fearing a lack of qualifications to address such issues. We are hopeful this resource will allow you to better minister to those elephants in your youth room.

We will discuss what appropriate intervention you, the youth minister, can give in these situations, and when to refer to other caring professionals. We will also help you do what you do best: provide a Catholic youth ministry response. You should be empowered to know that in a secular setting even the most competent mental health professionals cannot provide what you can: the healing presence of Christ Jesus.

What do you mean by "elephant?"

There is an old metaphor that comes from the family counseling profession about "The Elephant in the Living Room." The elephant is the family problem that everyone can see, but nobody does much, if anything, about. So, hoping it will go away, the family ignores the elephant. But problems, like elephants, can be quite big. And some baby elephants grow to become so big the room can barely contain them. Sometimes the elephant is so big it prevents you from seeing anything—or anyone—else.

Adolescents with problems beyond the normal challenges of growing up often bring their "elephants" with them in public. In youth ministry settings it is quite easy for a kid with emotional, family, or physical problems to act out or express their situations because of the comfort level. Your youth event may be the safest place in an adolescent's life. And you may see your share of elephants because kids know you and your team care.

If this is happening to you, congratulations, you're doing your job effectively. (We hear you now: "Some reward, huh?!") You are walking in the footsteps of a Christ that cared for all, especially those hurting and in need. If no one else has ever said it, allow us to say this right now: "Thank you." You need to hear that every now and then. Let this be both a pat on the back, and a gentle push to keep going.

What follows is helpful advice on how to continue ministering to "elephants" without getting stomped on or, at the very least, knee-deep in elephant poop. You will meet different kids with different problems. You will probably meet some familiar faces. We'll discuss what we see and give you a good guess about what you are seeing. Further, we'll offer some tips on how to provide an appropriate Catholic pastoral response.

You will not become a certified counselor by reading this book, nor an instant expert on adolescent psychology. You will, however, have a sharper eye and a better understanding of the amazing individuals God called you to serve.

One important disclaimer before we start to get our fingers dirty from all those icky teen problems: we do not heal, Christ heals. In *Renewing the Vision: A Framework for Catholic Youth Ministry*, the first sentence in the chapter on Pastoral Care reads: "The ministry of pastoral care is *a compassionate presence in imitation* of Jesus' care of people, especially those who were hurting and in need" (emphasis added). For some, the instinct is to fix what is broken. Pastoral care in youth ministry is a process in which we help a young person find a God who heals.

Using the synoptic Gospel of the healing of the Leper (Matthew 8:2-4; Mark 1:40-45; Luke 5:12-16), your job is not to heal the Leper, but to ensure the young person finds Christ on the way.

Chapter 1:

MEET THE ADOLESCENT BRAIN

"For I was…a stranger and you welcomed me."
(Matthew 25:35)

The alarm goes off at 5:45 am…6:00…6:15…

Mom has come in twice and last time she was clearly angry. It is now 6:45 and class begins at 7:30 am sharp. Finally, he summons up the energy to drag himself out of bed and into the bathroom. Breakfast is looking iffy at best.

The bathroom light is blinding, so it takes a few minutes to realize that the zit fairy has once again paid him a visit. His nose has a bump big enough to host the X Games. "The bullies in chemistry will have a field day," he reflects. "Chemistry, chemistry, CHEMISTRY! Oh @#%*! I didn't get my chemistry notebook finished, and I *know* Mr. So-and-so is going to do a notebook check today. He *hates* me anyway."

After a quick shower, he retreats to his bedroom and blasts his iPod speakers. The volume and musical genre are not popular with the family, but then, isn't that the point?

Showered, dressed, and rushed on yet another morning, our friend has forgotten that chemistry notebook, skipped a balanced breakfast, but did manage to balance six text message conversations. Breakfast is a Little Debbie and a Red Bull, and lunch will once again come out of the vending machine. Mom was yelling something about "practice after school and then blah, blah, blah."

The school is swarming at 7:27. Trying unsuccessfully to keep a low profile, a "friend" couldn't help but point out that facial blemish to anyone who would listen. The bell is ringing and Chemistry awaits. "Chemistry. Chemistry. Where is my chemistry notebook?"

"Mornings suck. FML," he thumbs into his phone as his Facebook status.

Just a typical day in the life of an adolescent brain.

Ch-Ch-Ch-Ch-Changes

Remember puberty? When the human body reaches a certain level of maturation, an amazing blossoming occurs that transforms the children of our species into fully functioning adults. Eventually.

As we all know first-hand (because we've all been there, no matter how hard we try to repress that phase), puberty is a frustrating experience for almost everybody who lives through it. It's fraught with the highs and lows of physical and emotional development. From a strictly biological standpoint, there is no more chaotic time in the human lifespan. The brain and body develop at varying stages, and that's why the Vatican declared that all middle school youth ministers are exempt from serving time in purgatory.

Well, actually that's an exaggeration. But feel free to place that in the suggestion box on your next trip to Rome.

Blame it on hormones, the little chemical messengers in the body that flip the switch on a new growth spurt of body parts and functions. From body hair to blemishes, voice changes to reproductive organs, every system in the body is getting new chemical information from its glands.

The brain is affected in this hormone wash. It changes the way young people process information and emotion. Adolescence is the time when our thinking goes from simple to complex. The young adolescent suddenly becomes an abstract thinker, capable of understanding, defining, and—for the first time—questioning life as an individual. The adolescent begins to question authority and conventional mores, and compares and contrasts conflicting viewpoints. Peer voices and opinions become increasingly important as the adolescent seeks validation from the community outside the home. Relationships are no longer arranged, but rather chosen.

From a religious perspective, expanding the power of the brain also means expanding the concept of God. The teen may question what God looks like, where and how God lives and works, or if God exists at all.

It is a liberation of sorts for the adolescent brain: it feels compelled to seek out freedom from family and anything attached to "being a kid." If you are nodding right now as you read this, you are a parent who can tell a story of that heartbreaking moment when your baby—whose life once revolved around you—wanted to be anyplace but home.

Be it your own child or someone else's, if you are in ministry with younger adolescents, they're changing. The child you once knew will quickly become a stranger. And you will welcome them, for yours is a work of mercy!

In fits and starts, eventually most young adolescents do break free, for better or worse. How healthy that foray into independence becomes is greatly influenced by the child's many social environments. With the Healing of the Leper gospel story still swimming in our souls, let's stretch the analogy: middle schools—and your middle school youth ministry—become a leper colony of sorts. How fortunate for us that we have God on our side!

The effects of puberty begin in early adolescence, and some theorize that the age of onset is decreasing into late childhood (10-12 years old), due to obesity.[1] What is undeniable is that younger adolescents in the United States and most western cultures are being exposed to grown-up images and situations at an earlier age that ever before, largely due to advances in digital communication. Even the strictest of parent has a difficult time shielding junior from all that the outside world has to offer as it streams in real-time in the palm of his hand.

---

1. Wattigney, Srinivasan, Chen, Greenlund, Berenson, "Secular trend of earlier onset of menarche with increasing obesity in black and white girls: the Bogalusa Heart Study." Secular trend of earlier onset of menarche.... Spring-Summer 1999. pubmed.gov/ PubMed U.S. National Library of Medicine . 25 March 2011 <http://www.ncbi.nlm.nih.gov/ pubmed/10421080>.

The actual starting point is different for everyone, another factor making middle school such an awkward place. If you were ever the tall girl, hairy guy, or the first girl with breasts (dollars to donuts you can name names to this day), you understand. The body growth influences appetite and sleep needs (ironically, the age group in most need of sleep gets the earliest school start). With an ever-increasing amount of elements stimulating the senses— cellular phones, internet, iPods, instant messaging, text messaging, social networking—it becomes a grind to fit it all in, and nearly impossible to do so by getting to bed at a decent hour.

In most cases the puberty monster has attacked the whole group by the last grade of middle school, but the growth process continues through the high school years and into college. Somewhere in this rough span of eight to ten years we also become exposed to the things that are deemed dangerous, taboo or sinful, most notably addictive substances and sex. Our morality—still unformed, and yet to be responsibly explored—is tested. Risks are taken. Consequences happen.

The Ripple Effect

Mark Twain remarked, "When a boy turns 13, seal him in a barrel and feed him through a knot hole. When he turns 16, plug up the hole." But you know the puberty-afflicted young people God called you to serve are not quarantined and kept in isolation, but instead just the opposite: they are waiting for you to bring them into a relationship with Jesus Christ. (They probably just don't know it yet!)

We give them curfews, allowances, cellular phones, and the keys to our car. The skill set of becoming a fully functional, social human being is forged in adolescence.

The amount of change on an adolescent—both physical and emotional—is felt not only by the afflicted, but by anyone that crosses his or her path (see: black cat). Youth ministers courageously stand there, convinced that they are sorely underpaid and underappreciated. Parents and family members are forced to weather the storm. There are usually more questions than answers.

If the rest of the family is well-adjusted and relatively problem-free and healthy the adolescent's "growing pains" are endured. But the complexity of issues facing the American family in the twenty-first century impact almost every family of every youth in your ministry: marriage success rates now hover below 50%, economic issues and pressures strain family functioning, health issues and overall stress deteriorate individuals and families, sudden tragedy shocks and numbs.

The likelihood of some of these life events deeply affecting an adolescent in your ministry is high. An adolescent who has good coping skills, a support system of friends and family, and is not debilitated by a disease or an addiction will generally manage to navigate the waters. For other teens they risk drowning.

> *Pastoral care is most fundamentally a relationship—a ministry of compassionate presence.*
> *~ Renewing the Vision, USCCB*

You are likely not a biologist, an expert on cognitive development, nor a psychologist. But what you are is a person hired to be in relationship with youth. What will make you an expert on the Ministry of Pastoral Care as detailed in *Renewing the Vision* isn't a scientific understanding of the adolescent brain, but rather a willingness to appreciate and understand its complexities as you faithfully walk the journey alongside the person carrying that noggin'.

The chapters that follow will address some of those events, and some common elephants stomping into youth rooms across the fruited plain. So gird your loins and prepare to fight the good fight! (1 Peter 1:13; 1 Timothy 6:12)

CHAPTER 2:

IT TAKES A VILLAGE: THE MANY WORLDS TEENS LIVE IN

"I urge you to live with all humility and gentleness, with patience, bearing with one another through love, striving to preserve the unity of the spirit through the bond of peace." (cf. Ephesians 4:2-3)

A long time ago, human beings figured out that living as family groups proved to be an excellent strategy for survival. Getting along with others and working cooperatively extended the tribe and helped us get to this point in history. Back then, the community was often defined by blood relations. Over the course of modern history, family has remained the primary unit, gathered together with other families in towns to share resources. But as technology and communication evolved, the communities grew larger and the world grew smaller.

Jesus taught us much about community. We know very little about his own family, but from what we can interpret in the Gospels we know that he was loved by parents that nurtured and supported him. We also know that when Jesus began his public ministry he knew that working with a small community of Apostles was an effective way to spread His Father's message. His disciples then spread the message of Christ to all corners of the globe. St. Paul evangelized one community at a time.

Modern humanity forms community in many different ways, and in many different sizes. At once we might belong to literally hundreds of overlapping communities, including family (in many forms), institution (school, work), and the ones formed by choice (friends, faith, Facebook). Adolescence is a time when a young person is beginning to choose their own communities as one way of shaping their own identity.

The young people to whom you minister are, like you, members of families, go to school or work, and are influencing and are being influenced by the world they experience. All of these relationships can and do change. While we seek to make the Gospel a positive and primary influence on their lives, we must appreciate that in a digital world today's teen will be influenced by many communities, for better or worse. Sometimes the interpersonal relationships developed in those communities can be negative (even destructive), and the impact on an adolescent can be substantial.

On any given night, your youth program gathers together teens from a dizzying network of social communities, no longer bound by physical attendance. It can be tricky to untangle, from a youth ministry perspective. We'll explore four communities that greatly impact adolescents: Family, School, Friends and Social Networks.

Family

Everyone has a different family. Each is unique. No two are alike. This is important to appreciate because when an adolescent is dealing with a family problem there are unique bonds that are in play, and we must avoid the temptation of jumping to any conclusions.

Research indicates that in recent years the parent-teen bond has become tighter: the term "helicopter parent" is often used to describe a parent who hovers over a child to ensure the child's safety and well-being. The parents of today's adolescents raised their children in a United States of America where we were successful in lobbying government and corporations to always think first about the children. We moved away from tough love toward compassion and inclusion. We enrolled them in organized sports ad nauseum, we stopped keeping score, and instead gave participation trophies so every child felt loved and supported. But as all this was going on, the family unit itself remained in disarray. Depending on which statistics you read, divorce rates have either climbed or remained steady, and as society became increasingly more transient, many of those divorced halves moved away.

In short, you know that many of the teens to which you minister do not have a family, they might have two or more.

This is important to remember because as youth ministers we are always communicating the "Family of God," and an adolescent's family situation will either enforce or contradict this.

We take for granted that Jesus Christ prayed to, spoke to, and was consubstantial with a loving and all-giving Father he called "Abba," a term of endearment. But a teen with an abusive or even distant father may struggle to identify with that relational aspect of our Trinitarian God.

Kevin tells the story of a teen—let's call her Rebecca—at the diocesan Lenten retreat he coordinates. The mountaintop experience of the retreat is the Reconciliation service. As we will mention often at our workshops and in this book, there is no single greater Catholic "program" that addresses hurting teens than the Sacrament of Reconciliation.

As we know, teens will rarely just show up an hour before Saturday Mass to go to confession. But when we present the sacrament within a supportive community, packaged with soft lighting, good music, and a message that speaks to the current life of a teen, he or she is much more likely to be immersed in the sacrament and feel the healing hand of Christ. And that's what Kevin was doing when Rebecca joined a hundred or so teens and adult youth leaders at that retreat.

The Examination of Conscience is done in an intentional way, using the Parable of the Prodigal Son and relating it to life as a modern day teenager. By this point in the weekend, Rebecca's small discussion group has established trust, and the group listens to the beautiful story told in Luke. Using the three primary characters in the story, teens consider the many ways in which they have fallen short of God's plan, and the examination leads the teens, literally, toward the arms of the loving Father that awaits them in the sacrament. The gathering hall is illuminated with an artist's painting of a loving embrace between the Prodigal Son and his father.

It was at this moment, Rebecca, clearly in need of healing, became visibly angry. For most teens, the thought of a loving embrace is comforting and therapeutic. For Rebecca it was a glaring reminder of the father she did not have: her parents had spent the better part of her life fighting over who would *not* have custody, a debate that ended when her father was incarcerated.

For the child from an unhealthy family environment, your youth ministry program and your extended parish community may be the most loving, nurturing family he or she experiences.

If you minister alongside teens long enough, you'll encounter a Rebecca or two. More often you'll encounter less extreme family stressors, things like job loss or gain, economic loss or gain, family member illness or death, normal transitions (going to new school), family member additions (birth, adoption, marriage, guardianship), abuse issues (physical, emotional, sexual), Substance abuse/dependency issues by one or more family members, a move, you get the idea.

There are some things to keep in mind. As a youth worker, you are mandated by law to report an allegation of abuse on a minor. Each state may have unique agencies to report to, or you may use the National Child Abuse Hotline (1-800-422-4453). Your parish or diocese may have specific policies for reporting as well. Know these policies before you have to. If you don't know who to call, simply contact your local police. They'll point you in the right direction.

One common thing we hear: "I'm afraid of betraying the confidence of my teen." Make it clear often—at many youth gatherings, not just retreats or "serious" discussion nights—that you accepted your call as a youth minister to help make them healthier, holier human beings, and part of that responsibility is ensuring their well-being.

"I will respect and honor the confidentiality of our relationship, with one notable exception: if you are subject to physical or emotional harm, by yourself or from someone else. Then I have the responsibility to care for you no matter what it takes."

This will make you a hero, not a pariah!

Most are aware that you have specific legal responsibilities, and most have probably encountered similar "disclaimers" at their schools already. While it does happen, few children lie about abuse. Chances are, if that teen is divulging information about harmful behavior, he or she is asking for help.

Another thing to keep in mind is that your own family experience does not apply to the person who is experiencing family problems. This is not a time to give advice. It is a time to listen to the young person.

And as you listen, always remember in any family experience there is always more than one side to every story. The adolescent is involved in the situation either passively or actively. You will not know the whole truth. But remember, providing pastoral care is not about fixing a problem, but rather about providing a healing presence of Christ.

Simply put, any strategy to reach out to youth must involve parents. If you consistently nurture relationship with parents today, making proactive efforts to communicate with parents personally, it will make life a lot easier when problems arise tomorrow.

School

The young people we serve spend most of their time in a world not of their making. Classes determine classmates and talents create cliques. Many of these groupings are now reinforced beyond the walls of the school yard with immediate Facebook status updates. The internet is written in ink, not in pencil, and reputations are created and ruined in lightning-fast 4G speeds. If they are blessed with gifted teachers (and you are one!), they will survive in this concrete jungle, and learn.

Some youth ministry programs draw primarily from a single school, but this is the exception rather than the rule. Most programs have teens from many schools: Catholic, public, private and charter, with home-schooled teens sprinkled in for good measure. This can be challenging—at times even heated (see: athletic rivalries)—but youth ministers should embrace these differences. Youth ministry should not simply be middle or high school with God mentioned occasionally, but rather a distinct and welcoming community that eliminates the worst of everyday school environments.

In the 80s, the term "peer pressure" was the overused buzz phrase of its day. While we don't hear it as often as we do today, rest assured it remains the single greatest influence on adolescent behavior. At the core of peer pressure is belonging. An adolescent seeks to belong to something as a means of shaping his or her identity.

Classes and school-sponsored sports and extracurricular activities, in a healthy expression, help young men and women share their God-given talents with the world and reinforce their importance in the world. At the same time, those activities can segment the population from one another and discourage interpersonal communication. In an unhealthy expression, they contradict the values of Christianity.

Make every effort to ensure that your program breaks down these walls that divide. Your teens should know—and be reminded often—that despite what they encounter in the hallways at school, they belong to a youth ministry program, a parish, and a faith that is one, holy, Catholic, and apostolic. They must be reminded often that we are all one in Christ Jesus (Galatians 3:28).

Seek out ways to place teens from different schools and different social strata alongside one another, and make affirmation a foundation of your program. Watching the point guard affirm the first chair of the violin section is liberating and most fundamentally Christian. Similarly, be ever-mindful that no matter how healthy your community might seem, those teens have been socialized to go right back to building walls. Be ready to step in and break down those walls when they form again.

School is hard enough for well-adjusted youth. But for young people with learning disabilities, physical or developmental challenges, or a hundred other obstacles to healthy social development, it can be a devastating experience with potentially life-altering repercussions.

You likely have little control over what happens at school. But you do have the power to influence the teens you serve, and to empower them to live out the Gospel when they leave your program. Inspire them to go to all corners of their schools and make disciples.

Friends (the ol' fashioned, flesh-and-blood kind)

As we grow into fully-functioning adults living in the world, along with physical maturation, somewhere along the way we learn the ability to relate with others. For some this is easy, for others, not so easy.

The teens we serve fall along the spectrum between introversion (shy, inward) and extroversion (outgoing). Their confidence is buoyed by successfully engaging in social interactions, and embarrassments are either overcome or reinforced.

And along that journey, they make friends. How it happens sometimes only God fully knows. But it happens. Further, they move in and out of friendships, too. Sometimes this happens in the course of a week, leaving you, the youth minister to deal with the fallout and drama. Nonetheless, God created human beings for relationships. God desires that we are in relationship with our Creator, and all of God's Creation, specifically each other.

When it comes to teens, we know that they not only form friendships, they are often defined by their friendships. And, let's face it, we adults carefully scrutinize their circle of friends.

For the purposes of this section, we'll first address the term "friend" as a person-to-person, interpersonal, and very much flesh and blood relationship. Facebook has redefined the term "friend," but despite living in a digital world in which they might have contact with hundreds of acquaintances, they still gather together in much smaller clusters.

I am reminded of an episode of "The Simpsons" with a scene showing senior citizens outside the Springfield Retirement Castle. Rarely participating in the "outside world," upon their walking outside one of them proclaims, "I don't like the looks of those teenagers," and they all scurry inside.

In one short scene, the writers communicated in a funny, satirical way much about our young people, the way we view them, and the way in which they form community. The landscape of American summers is filled with parking lots, gas stations, and fast food restaurants packed with teens just hanging out. Sure, some of these teens are up to no good, but by definition, they are forming community.

So, let's examine that: a group of peers that gather together at a defined location, sharing common bonds, speaking openly about their joys and hurts, triumphs and frustrations, enjoying a welcoming atmosphere in which they are loved and supported. Is that not the mission of our parish?!

As youth ministers we must accept and acknowledge the cluster mentality of youth, and embrace it. But we also must challenge it: creating safe and rewarding gathering environments. We should not think negatively about a small group of teens that gather together in community, but rather work toward bringing together many different kinds of so-called "cliques" in a spirit of connectedness.

We adult types often criticize cliques and justifiably discourage teens from forming them. The word "clique" has a very negative connotation. But if we're honest with ourselves, we recognize that teens aren't the only ones who form cliques! We might label a destructive group a clique, but label a group with more positive intentions a "small community." The fact is, in our culture we are all inclined to form small communities that share like interests and personalities. We mention this because we have seen all too often that other adults in the parish community look upon the group of adult youth ministry leaders as a clique! Remember it is natural for teens to form small communities, and the small communities aren't bad in and of themselves. It is only when these groups become exclusive that they become a detriment to the proclamation of the Christian mission.

The difference between the cliques that form amongst the teens in your program and the cliques they form at school is that you will hold them accountable for negative or destructive behavior that doesn't protect the dignity of the human person, including and especially bullying.

Facebook Friends

If Jesus came back to us in the flesh today, would he say, "There is no greater love than to lay down one's life for a Facebook friend?" (a curious adaptation of John 15:13)

We have seen powerful evangelization through social networking: teens and youth ministry leaders nationally and locally using tweets and Facebook posts to spread God's love using new media. Sadly, humankind is also sinful, and we've also seen social media used in very harmful ways.

In any form of social interaction the risk of bullying exists, and we know that with the power of internet social networking, bullying can take place at anytime, sometimes without fear of repercussion. It seems almost daily we are reading sad tales of teens committing suicide because of bullying.

Facebook should not be avoided in ministry. Just the opposite—it should be embraced as an effective means of communication, promotion, and evangelization. Such social networking gives youth ministers access to teens they never had before, for better or worse.

In the same way you would hold teens accountable at your youth gatherings, your teens should be held accountable for their behavior online. Make sure your teens know that they are an integral part of your program, and as such you will hold them to a higher standard because that's what God does. Make your ministry a bully-free zone in which the dignity of every human being will be protected and affirmed, and that extends online, as well.

While we're on the topic of Facebook, recognize that bullying isn't the only evil that you will find on those walls. You are bound to encounter in a very real way the daily challenges of life as an American teenager. Simply put, you have been given a window into the world of the teens you serve.

While there are inherent evils associated with social networking and other forms of internet communication, let's look at the glass as half-full, shall we? Remember in the late 90s when we were worried that teens were hiding from the outside world, alone on their computers, worried that they had been engulfed by our overly individualistic culture? Look at the way teens use media today: they seek to share their lives with others, they seek to engage with others (even strangers). Even if they're not talking with others, they're very often thumbing out a text message or checking Facebook on their phones. They are always in community.

We strongly encourage youth ministers to carefully utilize social media to improve or enhance your relational ministry. Consult your diocesan guidelines on such matters, and clearly communicate with parents your intentions to use Facebook in your ministry.

If you chuckled at the thought of laying down your life for a Facebook friend, you subtly acknowledged what the teens you serve may or may not realize having been formed in a world always connected by the web: there is a very important social distinction between live, face-to-face communications and communications that take place electronically.

We belong to a Sacramental Church that has real, tangible signs of Christ's presence in the world. Ours is a faith that appeals to the senses. We like the way we can feel, see, smell, and wrap our arms around the Almighty! We would not be content to read about the True Presence of Eucharist, but rather we are drawn toward it; we are drawn toward a very real encounter with Christ, and we encounter Christ when two or more are gathered (Matthew 18:20).

We have to reinforce to the teens we serve that Christ calls us to such a real, flesh-and-blood community. Social networking has expanded our understanding of community, and it's also given us an effective and efficient way of reaching out to a large amount of teenagers. Make every effort to ensure that your social networking is used as a tool to bring those you serve into real encounters with Christ through the gathered community.

Pastoral Response

We can remember a time when youth ministers used to be jealous of Catholic high school campus ministers because they had so much more access to teens. "Think of how effective I could be as a youth minister if I saw them more than once a week!" we would tell ourselves.

With the help of modern technology we now have a constant stream of information about and communication with teens, their friends, and families. For better or worse, we now have a clear window into their Monday through Saturday world, and sometimes it isn't pretty. But it is real, and now we have a way to bring the light of Christ into their many worlds in many ways.

Some suggestions:

- **Meet them everywhere, but know and embrace your diocese's safe environment and internet policies.** We acknowledge that it can seem at times like we have to jump through hoops for the right and privilege to wash the feet of teens. But know that those policies are there for the health and safety of those teens we love. In recent years many dioceses have also adopted internet communications guidelines and policies as well. Know the policies, and hold each other accountable.

  Utilize internet and cellular technology to enhance your evangelization efforts and live out Jesus' call to build His Church! But do so responsibly.

  If your diocese does not have any formal policies regarding internet communications, consult the Recommended Technology Guidelines for Pastoral Work with Young People, developed by the National Federation for Catholic Youth Ministry in consultation with the USCCB Secretariat for Child and Youth Protection and the Secretariat for Laity, Marriage, Family Life and Youth. (www.nfcym.org/resources/technology/index.htm)

- **Include parents in your ministry programming.** It's time to go beyond the "parent meeting," and actively engage parents in your youth programs. Have a retreat for parents only, or with teens and parents together. Offer a workshop on faith and parenting. Invite parents to join for portions of your gatherings or prayer services. Surprise teens with letters from parents while on retreats. Send periodic emails or letters that give summary reports about the ministry. Most of all, talk to parents! While youth gather, the youth ministry team should intentionally greet youth while allowing the coordinator to be in the parking lot greeting parents.

- **Go to school.** Make every effort to be physically present at the schools of the youth you serve. This will reinforce our challenge to be "in the world, but not of the world" (cf. John 15:18-19). It is easy for the teens you serve to be Christian in the moment at your events, activities, and gatherings. It's not so easy when they are surrounded by their secular world and their school friends outside of your youth programs. Youth ministers are always youth ministers, whether you see teens at church, at the grocery store, or at high school football games. Attend sports, plays, and concerts. Go to your school activity coordinator and ask to volunteer at dances or field trips. Some allow you to visit for lunch. You don't have to preach, just be an ever-present face of Christ, encouraging them to do the same.

CHAPTER 3:

THE DARK SIDE OF THE ADOLESCENT BRAIN: ANXIETY, DEPRESSION & SUICIDE

"The light shines in the darkness, and the darkness has not overcome it." (John 1:5)

As the throngs tripped over one another to get to the pizza boxes, you overheard a small group of chatty girls. "Maryellen has been acting strange lately. What's her deal?" Come to think of it, you hadn't seen Maryellen around much.

"I should get in touch with her," you told yourself. But then, you tell yourself that at least three times a day.

She slips your mind until you see her at lunch at the mall food court in the middle of a school day. And she has indeed changed. She looks embarrassed to see you, but she comes by your table to say hello.

The conversation that ensues isn't unlike most conversations you have with teens when you bump into them in the community:

"How are you?"
"Fine."
"How are things?"
"O.K."
"We miss you, you should come next week, we'd love to see you."

This is followed by a polite nod to needing to get back to something else, but this time you sense that Maryellen wants to say more. Tears well up in her eyes.

> The story at the beginning of this chapter also illustrates a key lesson in youth ministry: we are always on call! Always remember that no matter where you go, whether it is on official church business or not, you represent St. Your-Church, and, by extension, the Holy Roman Catholic Church! In the same way we urge teens to live out the Gospel between Sundays, we too are called to live lives of integrity, ever-mindful that we are the face of God whether we're at a youth ministry function, a high school football game, the mall, or the local bar and grill.

Status: Stressed

At this moment in time you are reading this book, God bless you, but you are also occupying a particular point on any number of scales. You might not have noticed, but you are.

You are somewhere on a point between robust health and chronic illness. You are in any number of functioning or fractured relationships. Your challenges are invigorating, manageable or overwhelming to you. You see life as positive or negative or shades in between. This place you occupy on all these scales is your *status*, your place in life.

If no other factors impacted you and your place on all these scales, one would hope that all will be just fine. But things do affect us. Some things are events, changes in life. Some events are in our control, most events are beyond our control. The positive or negative force applied by these events is felt as stress. Stress is best understood not as the events that we endure but rather our physical and mental reaction to the events.

Many very positive events in life are stressful. Let's use the analogy of a roller coaster: think about the emotions you feel throughout the experience, from the fear you battle standing in line to the sheer exhilaration of the ride, to the sense of pride you feel when you've conquered the challenge! Your body's senses are heightened, the adrenaline flows, your heart pounds, your mental, emotional and physical limitations are challenged.

We like to be scared, but only to an extent. If it was almost your turn to climb in the car but you saw ambulances and a triage unit standing by the exit, you might think twice about riding. But instead, you see others leaving the ride under their own power, smiling and laughing, and you know that whatever negative emotions are rushing through your body, it will be brief, and you, too, will feel that same joy on the other end.

As long as the stressor (the event) is temporary, the body can endure the physical sensations, and, with a little rest, recover just fine. But if the stressor lasts too long—a prolonged illness or family crisis-induced stress, for example—the body begins to wear down. And as the body goes, the brain follows. Thoughts can become melancholy, moods can darken. Depression looms.

Adolescence can be a prolonged stressful event for some members of your youth ministry program. As discussed earlier, the new flow of hormones alone can account for some of the erratic moods we find in adolescents. But we keenly remember the impact of life events.

Tipping Point

When the capacity to cope is diminished—the most common culprits are illness, poor diet, diminished or disturbed sleep patterns, and tragedy—the body and brain will usually break down. To what degree and for how long is the stuff of diagnosis: it could be the difference between a bad mood and clinical depression, or the difference between nervousness and an anxiety disorder.

Feeling better is clearly everyone's goal. But *getting* better is healing. Adolescents are in the psychological framework to pursue the former. For many teens, self-medicating becomes the easiest (and riskiest) way to feel better.

In the age of constantly-flowing information and communication, it is very difficult for teens to turn off their electronic devices and rest. It is no surprise that highly-caffeinated energy drinks have become the beverage of choice for sleep-deprived teens. This is an example of a teen finding a drug—albeit a legal one—to fix their problem, rather than seek out the proper means of healing.

Anxiety, Depression, & Suicide

When we discuss changes in mood we need to remember that anxiety and depression are related; both are reactions when stress exceeds a tipping point.

Anxiety is common with teens, particularly amongst high school upperclassmen, and this anxiety is often stress-induced. Teens are under immense pressure to get into a college of their choice, and they are under pressure to pursue scholarships that can help pay for it. For young adults who forego college, they face a very challenging job market, or the prospects of serving a nation in a time of war. Today's high school extracurricular activities, most notably high-profile sports, are increasingly demanding of a teen's limited time and his or her family's limited financial resources. Today's teen has grown up participating in nonstop organized activities, but now when those daily practices are over, the homework is lengthier and more difficult, he or she is exploring dating relationships, and perhaps trying to earn money at a job to pay for that car.

Oh, yeah, and we want them to come to youth group, too.

Other teens will be suffering through a traumatic event, and their anxiety is considered *Acute* or *Post Traumatic*.

By now you're used to seeing teens—and your team of leaders—who are stressed out. Your gatherings probably feel like support groups sometimes! But sometimes someone we serve becomes overwhelmed, and his or her normal coping mechanisms break down. It is then when additional help is needed.

Utilize the accompanying information from the American Psychiatric Association to know what to look for.

Symptoms of Anxiety/Panic Attack:

"A discrete period of intense fear or discomfort in the absence of real danger that is accompanied by at least 4 of 13 somatic or cognitive symptoms (including): palpitations, sweating, trembling or shaking, sensations of shortness of breath or smothering, feeling of choking, chest pain or discomfort, nausea or abdominal distress, dizziness or lightheadedness, derealization or dispersonalization, fear of losing control or 'going crazy," fear of dying, paresthesias, and chills or hot flashes. The attack has a sudden onset and builds to a peak rapidly (usually in 10 minutes or less) and is often accompanied by a sense of imminent danger or impending doom and an urge to escape.

(DSM-IV-TR, American Psychiatric Assoc., Arlington, VA, 2000, p 430)

Many of these symptoms mimic serious medical issues, including but not limited to heart attack and asthma. If anyone experiences these symptoms at a youth ministry event, err on the side of caution, and seek medical assistance immediately.

Symptoms of Major Depressive Episode:

"Five or more of the following symptoms have been present during the same 2-week period and represent a change from previous functioning; at least one of the symptoms is either (1) depressed mood or (2) loss of interest or pleasure:

1. depressed mood most of the day, nearly every day (in adolescents, can be irritable mood)
2. markedly diminished interest or pleasure in all, or almost all, activities most of the day, nearly every day
3. significant weight loss when not dieting or weight gain or decrease or increase in appetite
4. insomnia or hypersomnia nearly every day
5. psychomotor agitation or retardation (lack of muscle control) nearly every day
6. fatigue or loss of energy nearly every day
7. feelings of worthlessness or excessive or inappropriate guilt nearly every day
8. diminished ability to think or concentrate, or indecisiveness, nearly every day
9. recurrent thoughts of death, recurrent suicidal ideation without a specific plan, or a suicide attempt or a specific plan for committing suicide

(DSM-IV-TR, American Psychiatric Assoc., Arlington, VA, 2000, p 356)

If these Anxiety/Depression symptoms persist (two weeks for depression): the young person should be encouraged to seek help on a therapeutic level.

A quick discussion about Depression and Suicide Ideation is in order here. Most adolescents have thought about their own death; it is the mark of a brain that has begun to think on an abstract level. Adolescents suffering through depression may be more inclined to focus on suicidal thoughts. One of the most-discussed topics at our workshops on teens in crisis is distinguishing between a severely-depressed teen and a suicidal teen.

Determining what you should do when those elephants start stomping around your parish grounds can best be addressed with three key *don'ts*:

1. **Don't think you know the person's problem before you ask the questions.** As hard as it may be to ask the tough questions, it's even harder on the young person answering them. Give them time and listen carefully. As a rule of thumb, use about half as many words as the person you are speaking with, and embrace silence and compassionate eye contact. The Spirit resides in that silence, so check the urge to fill it with advice.

2. **Don't ask a closed question.** A closed question is any question that can be answered with a one word answer. "Are you O.K.?" is perhaps the most often used closed question. "You seem depressed, are you O.K.?" would be an example of breaking both the first and second "don't."

So what are possible open questions you can ask?
Here are a few examples:

- "I noticed _____ has been different in your life lately. What's going on?"
- "I heard about _____ that you are dealing with. How are you coping with_____?"
- "I was sorry to hear about_____. How are you doing?"
- "It seems you have had something on your mind lately. What are thinking about?"

Always ask for more detail if you don't understand their problem. Keep in mind these vital points:

- As a youth minister, you are mandated by state/federal law to report an allegation of abuse. This is not an option. Know your state's laws, especially if you are the coordinator.

- Too many youth ministers avoid addressing the tough topics or asking the tough questions because they feel they lack counseling skills. You don't have to be a licensed counselor to care! You don't need an expensive degree on your wall to listen. In fact, you have one skill many counselors lack: the ability to pray with those hurting teens. However, you will likely encounter situations that require the assistance of a professional. The old adage applies here: "When in doubt, refer out."

- If intervention is needed, have a resource list ready. In fact, it's always a good idea to use a pre-emptive strategy here: have a list of referrals ready, because it's not a matter of if pastoral care issues will surface, but when. For your convenience, use the *Pastoral Care Resource List* (found on page 83). The right side of that page will require some advanced planning on your part, but when lives are on the line you will be glad you took the time to complete it.

3. **Don't be alone with youth**. One good youth ministry skill to have is to know how to be one-on-one with a teen without really being alone. Have a mapped-out plan in place with other adult leaders on your team that allows you to ensure a safe, comfortable environment without placing you at risk. Everyone on your leadership team should be in compliance with your diocese's Safe Environment policy.

The conventional wisdom has always been to avoid bringing up the topic of suicide with the depressed teen, lest you put "thoughts in their head". That conventional wisdom is WRONG. The opposite is usually true: you may be the first person who is acknowledging it out loud.

If you suspect a teen is suicidal, ask the following three questions:
"Are you thinking about killing yourself?"
"Do you have a plan?" (How they will do it)
"Do you have the means to carry it out?" (weapon, pills, etc.)

If a young person answers two or more of those questions with a "yes," you should consider him or her at risk. You should immediately encourage professional help with both the adolescent and, when possible, his or her parent or guardian.

Pastoral Response

When we encounter depressed teens and teens in crisis situations, we realize that Catholic youth ministry is about so much more than pizza and volleyball. It is about walking the journey with teens through rough terrain, and it is truly about being the face of Christ for young people when they need to see the face of Christ the most.

Youth ministry must always be fun! They are teens, after all. But as we build relationships with God's young Church, we owe it to them to become intimately aware of the baggage they carry, and to understand that if we have them check those bags at the door, we have done them a great injustice.

We must be willing to stretch beyond our own comfort zone, embrace the hurt, and call attention to those elephants in the room. We are inspired by Paul's letter to the Corinthians in which he likens the community to the body and its many parts:

But as it is, there are many parts, yet one body. The eye cannot say to the hand, "I do not need you," nor again the head to the feet, "I do not need you." Indeed, the parts of the body that seem to be weaker are all the more necessary, and those parts of the body that we consider less honorable we surround with greater honor, and our less presentable parts are treated with greater propriety, whereas our more presentable parts do not need this. But God has so constructed the body as to give greater honor to a part that is without it, so that there may be no division in the body, but that the parts may have the same concern for one another. If (one) part suffers, all the parts suffer with it; if one part is honored, all the parts share its joy. (1 Corinthians 12:20-26)

You owe it to the hurting teen to find healing through your community.

In his Confessions, Saint Augustine wrote to God, "You have made us for yourself, and our hearts are restless till they find their rest in you." Teens often feel that something is missing in their life, and too often they seek healing in very unhealthy ways.

You, the youth minister, have an incredible gift: the power to give a hurting teen the only real thing that provides that kind of rest and comfort that Augustine wrote about. Seek ways to acknowledge and address the many issues and challenges that your teens face, and you will find that your youth ministry program will fill a void in teens' lives they simply cannot find in their secular world.

Some suggestions:

- **Seek out a licensed counselor, and have him or her on "retainer."** You may find there is a parishioner in your community with that expensive degree. In the spirit of true stewardship, ask him or her to consider sharing those talents with your ministry for free or at a significantly reduced cost.

- **Work with community organizations to provide speakers and presentations**. Some of these organizations are funded with grant money and are searching for youth programs like yours to share their message. Trust the experts.

- **Embrace the Sacrament of Reconciliation.** There is simply no better way to provide a truly Catholic response for hurting teens than to give them the kind of healing that is present in the Sacrament of Reconciliation.

- **Pray with teens.** Get in the habit of praying with teens. There will be difficult conversations, and while you always plan to follow up on the teen tomorrow, next week, and weeks after, the conversation has to end, at least for now. There is no better way to end the conversation than this:

"We've talked about a lot of big stuff here, and thank you for trusting me/us enough with your burden. I have to be honest, I/we will try to do everything possible to help you, but you know we're not alone in this!

I/we really want to close tonight by praying with you and asking the Holy Spirit to guide us."

Have the teen bow his or her head and embrace quiet for a minute or two. Promise the young person that you will continue to pray.

Life Teen Resources

The following Life Nights address the topics of depression and suicide within a youth group setting:
- Push-Up Pop
- Cut to the Heart

All Life Teen resources can be downloaded by subscribing parishes at www.catholicyouthministry.com

CHAPTER 4:

PAY ATTENTION! ATTENTION DEFICITS AND BEHAVIOR ISSUES

> "When he returned he found them asleep. He said to Peter, "Simon, are you asleep? Could you not keep watch for one hour? Watch and pray that you may not undergo the test. The spirit is willing but the flesh is weak." (Mark 14:37-38)

We, servants of Christ's adolescent Church family, know what *nodding off* looks like. We should be the first to admit our own guilt: we have all drifted off the attention highway from time to time, whether it be a quick loss of focus, a brief daydream, or the full-on power nap. (May the Lord help you if the latter should occur during a staff meeting!) Our hearts are in the right place, we're just tired.

But we know kids who seem to *always* be in la-la-land. They are either wired and bouncing off the walls, or nearly comatose. Sometimes these behaviors are easily explained by circumstances. Anyone who has ever led an overnight retreat knows about the roller coaster of emotions and attitudes that result from sleep-deprivation. Anyone who has ever attended a World Youth Day Papal Vigil, overnight and Mass has encountered that one hundred fold. But when there are kids who seem to consistently act out within your ministry, it is important to understand why.

Attention Disorders

"Jordan never stops moving," your exasperated 7th grade catechist complains.

"He fidgets constantly, like he is *on* something."

Actually the problem isn't that Jordan is *on something*, it is in fact just the opposite. Jordan is medicated for ADHD (Attention Deficit Hyperactivity Disorder), but only on school days. So by Sunday, he is the most symptomatic he will be for the entire week.

Please note that this is not the forum to debate whether or not children are properly diagnosed with ADHD. For every study indicating there are too many children medicated for the condition there is another indicating that many children who do in fact have ADHD aren't receiving treatment. Regardless, in the last thirty years there has been a sharp increase in the percentage of children diagnosed with ADHD, and as a result, the number of children receiving ADHD medication has also increased.

Your job as youth minister, of course, is not to determine whether or not a child should or should not be on the medication. But in some circumstances it behooves you to know if a child is on such medication.

Those pesky permission forms are your friend!

Our combined years of Youth Ministry experience have taught us there are a few absolutes to running youth ministry but here is one: *read your health forms!*

In addition to knowing a child's allergies, it serves us well to know if he/she is regularly taking a medication. Please remember everyone's medical information is private and protected by law. You may share information only with those who directly work with that child, and only with parent's permission.

In matters related to the distribution and intake of medicine, always follow diocesan policies, guidelines, and recommendations. For regular gatherings of a few hours, this is usually not a problem. But if you take a mission trip, go away on a retreat, or even attend a day-long youth rally, you are bound to encounter a teen who needs to stay on his or her dosing schedule. Know in advance if that child is allowed to self-medicate. For fear of liability, schools and youth-serving agencies have increasingly chosen to steer clear of any and all distribution of drugs. We must balance this fear with a knowledge that we wish to bring all of God's children to our ministry, and we cannot rule out a child because he or she may need medication.

A few phone calls or emails to your diocesan youth ministry director, risk-management representative, and parents on Tuesday could save you a lot of frustration and confusion during the weekend. The old phrase "know before you go" should not only apply to you, the youth minister, but also to the parents.

With that in mind, it is good to know if a kid in your group is on or off their meds when they are in your care.

There are two diagnosed disorders that we call ADD/ADHD, or Attention Deficit Disorder/Attention Deficit Hyperactivity Disorder: an Inattentive type—one that is observed as "spaced-out" behaviors—and Hyperactive/Impulsive type, observed as "hyper" behaviors. Consult the information from the American Psychiatric Association in the box on this page to see if any of your teens might fit into one of these categories.

Symptoms of Attention-Deficit/Hyperactivity Disorder:

Inattentive type: Six (or more) of the following, persisting for at least six months to a degree that is maladaptive and inconsistent with developmental level:
- Often fails to give close attention to details or makes careless mistakes in schoolwork, work, or other activities
- often has difficulty sustaining attention in tasks or play activities
- often does not seem to listen when spoken to directly
- often does not follow through on instructions and fails to finish schoolwork, chores or duties in the workplace

- often has difficulties organizing tasks and activities
- often avoids, dislikes or is reluctant to engage in tasks that require sustained mental effort (such as schoolwork or homework)
- often loses things necessary for tasks or activities (e.g. toys, school assignments, pencils, books, tools)
- is often easily distracted by extraneous stimuli
- is often forgetful in daily activities.

Hyperactive/Impulsive type: Six (or more) of the following, persisting for at least six months to a degree that is maladaptive and inconsistent with developmental level:

Hyperactivity
- Often fidgets with hands or feet or squirms in seat
- often leaves seat in classroom or in other situations in which remaining seated is expected
- often runs about or climbs excessively in situations in which it is inappropriate (in adolescents or adults, may be limited to subjective feelings of restlessness)
- often has difficulty playing or engaging in leisure activities quietly
- is often "on the go" or often acts as if "driven by a motor"
- often talks excessively.

Impulsivity
- Often blurts out answers before questions have completed
- often has difficulty awaiting turn
- often interrupts or intrudes on others (e.g. butts into conversations or games)

(DSM-IV-TR, American Psychiatric Assoc., Arlington, VA, 2000, p 92)

Remember the first time you took your toddler to Disney World and he was bouncing off the walls and couldn't sleep? You probably said, "He's overstimulated."

Both Inattentive Hyperactive/Impulsive types of ADD/ADHD are physical symptoms of, believe it or not, an *understimulated* region of the brain. And both types have been treated medically with stimulant based-medications for decades, as some of us in youth ministry know firsthand.

While it's true in some cases that ADD/ADHD has been misdiagnosed, whenever you become aware that a child is being treated for it, you should proceed with the assumption that the child does indeed have ADD/ADHD, make every effort to ensure the child is following the proper dosing schedule while in your care, and plan accordingly.

Oppositional Defiant Disorders (ODD)

Unfortunately, in some cases the behavior of the child exceeds disruptive and becomes downright defiant. Known as Conduct Disorders or Oppositional Defiant Disorders (ODD), a child becomes openly uncooperative or even hostile toward authority figures. Oppositional behavior is actually considered a normal part of early adolescent behavior (aren't *you* lucky, middle school youth ministers!), but when the defiance becomes so extreme it interferes with the child's ability to function normally in even low-stress environments, that child may have ODD.

There will be moments in ministry where teens will not like what you have to say. There will be teens that do not get along with other teens. But if one particular child demonstrates consistent behavior that becomes demonstrative, argumentative and outwardly defiant—with you or his or her peers—you should contact his or her parents as soon as possible. You should know in advance that a child with ODD seeks out conflict, and any ensuing argument—especially in public—will result in you, the youth minister, being ultimately more upset than the young person.

Do your best to diffuse the bomb by refusing to surrender to anger. In most cases the youth with ODD seeks out conflict with his or her peers as well, so the other teens are looking to you for guidance on how to handle him or her. No one expects you to be a behavioral psychologist—let the parents seek out treatment—but this is yet another opportunity to turn a cheek, "love your enemy," and demonstrate a compassionate, loving presence of Christ.

Complicating matters even further? Biology. Give anyone in middle school ministry an honorary medical degree and he or she will diagnose all of the young people with ADD/ADHD.

The lines between inappropriate behavior and healthy boundary-testing are blurred in early adolescence, and every middle school minister goes home at night and wonders if he or she was too tough, or not tough enough.

Symptoms of ODD include:
- Frequent temper tantrums
- Excessive arguing with adults
- Active defiance and refusal to comply with adult requests and rules
- Deliberate attempts to annoy or upset people
- Blaming others for his or her mistakes or misbehavior
- Frequent anger and resentment
- Spiteful attitude and revenge seeking

Courtesy American Academy of Child Adolescent Psychiatry

Justin: a case study

We present to you our case study: "Justin." There's a Justin in every parish.

Justin is infamous in the annals of your parish. He was caught swiping doughnuts in the parish hall at age 9 and was kicked out of the altar servers because he tried to sample unconsecrated wine at 12. But Justin's mom is the chair of the annual Giving Tree, and Justin's dad is on the Parish Council, and both are insistent that Justin be as passionate about their parish and faith as they are. So they "strongly encourage" him to participate in youth ministry. (And by "strongly encourage," they mean, "We're fairly confident after we drop you off that you won't make the four mile walk home through the cold and snow.")

It doesn't take a psychologist to know that Justin's bad attitude and frequent misbehavior are his way of proclaiming to the world that "church is not my thing." It's also very likely he's hurting about something.

But your challenge remains: bring Justin into a relationship with Christ.

There is perhaps no greater time in life than adolescence where rapid change occurs, most notably in middle school years. A child begins to mature physically, then emotionally, and with the right guidance, behaviorally (but not always in that order). Where faith fits in is a crapshoot at best!

We also know that adolescents are having to grow up faster than ever. A phenomenon known as age compression, issues that were once unique to high school youth are now being experienced in early adolescence.

Sadly, a healthy number of churches today fulfill their mandate to catechize these students for an hour or so and send them on their way with, "See you in class next week."

That your parish has established youth ministry as a priority is a good start—it's a recognition that there is more to a holistic experience of faith formation than teaching facts from the Catechism. Now it's up to you and your team to form the entire person of Justin, not just his brain.

You and your ministry may be the opportunity for change in Justin's life, provided you remember your relational ministry skills.

You must start with replacing "See you next week," with "How are you?"

You want to walk the journey with Justin. But he first has to allow you to join him on his journey. That won't happen until you're prepared to ask "How are you?" and really mean it.

Justin needs an "I believe in you," an "I refuse to back off, no matter what you do," and perhaps even more he needs a *thing* to do.

Ministry lessons from St. Paul

Pull any book about saints or popes or any holy people off the shelf, or pull up saintsorpopesoranyholypeople.com (I'm pretty sure that website doesn't exist, but you get the point). Scan anyone's bio, and within the first paragraph or two you'll read about what he or she DID.

Saint Paul knew that each Christian community was dependent on many people with many different charisms working together as a functioning body (1 Corinthians 12:27-31). And don't think for a second that there weren't a few Justins in Corinth. Seriously, Google the history of Corinth. Justin's doughnut heist would have barely been noticed.

Two thousand years of spreading Christianity to all corners of the globe could not have been accomplished without transforming the souls of a few bad seeds. Heck, forget about the people Paul was trying to transform and think about his own transformation.

If Justin does indeed suffer from an attention disorder, you and your team will have your work cut out for you. See the "symptom" boxes included in this chapter for a list of what challenges you should expect.

But there is no nobler task than the transformation of your Justin, and it will start by helping Justin find his Christian charism. Then and only then can you engage Justin in that two thousand year old Christian mission.

Perhaps "engage" is a bad verb. Let's try "immerse" on for size. Paul likely heard an engaging story or two about Jesus, but only when he was immersed in the presence of Christ was he transformed. So, too, we must find a way to immerse Justin.

Even then the transformation will not cure him of his disorder. The symptoms and challenges remain. To borrow from Luke, we will walk that road—it might be slow and rocky at times—and be patient, hoping that in God's time he will recognize, and feel his heart burning. (Luke 24:13-35)

Pastoral Response

We hear often, "Why do young people disappear after Confirmation?" Even in parishes with vibrant youth ministry, a significant number of teens fade away. So while this chapter addresses youth who, for whatever reason, are disengaged, let's first thank God that we have them there at all! Yes, ministry would be a lot easier without them. But you and I both know that God calls us to something much more noble!

Some suggestions:

- **Engage them.** Traditional top-down, teacher/authority/adult-speaks-youth-listen models of formation are increasingly difficult to handle for a generation entitled to an opinion on everything. In the same way social networking has conditioned them to comment on posts, photos and videos, and "like" or "tag" virtually anything that piques their curiosity, so, too, will they desire to interact with the Gospel and our Catholic teaching. Opinions don't have to be "right," but they have to be shared.

- **Employ them.** See the Justin case study above. You've done a great job recruiting adult leaders. But youth ministry is *their* ministry, after all. Let them invest some human capital in their company.

Do not harbor any unrealistic expectations that by giving such teens tasks and responsibilities that their attention deficits will disappear. But unlike others who are not as loving, patient, and kind as you, the youth minister, you are doing the right thing. Give a task and allow him or her to sink or swim, but be ready to toss a life preserver so he or she doesn't drown.

Too often when we think of youth leaders we envision the straight-A student, the teen who would never misbehave, and certainly never steal doughnuts. Let's be honest, that kid is much easier to manage!

But Jesus left the church in the hands of young men who looked a lot like Justin, and here we are today. In eight years, we want to see Justin on your Core Team!

- **Invite, invite, invite.** One of the most important things to remember when ministering to a young person who is emotionally, spiritually, or mentally detached from whatever program you are leading is the power of the invitation. Even if teens have already made it clear that they want no part in youth ministry, or they are there but disengaged, continue to invite. Eventually they will be cured of the "disease" of being a teenager, and later in life when they think about the Holy Roman Catholic Church they will remember your smiling face and invitation. See? That's why we don't judge our youth ministry success by how many teens show up for our activities!

- **Consult a behavioral specialist.** If you are in a situation in which you will be in ministry for a prolonged period of time with a young person with a child demonstrating any of the behavioral disorders described in this chapter, don't go it alone. Consult with a professional for advice.

CHAPTER 5:
MINISTERING TO TEENS WITH SPECIAL NEEDS

"Indeed, the parts of the body that seem to be weaker are all the more necessary, and those parts of the body that we consider less honorable we surround with greater honor." (1 Corinthians 12:22-23)

Every so often your ministry will be blessed by the involvement of a teen with special needs. One of Jim's lasting memories in his aeons of ministry is the memory of Danny.

Danny entered Jim's program among a relentless freshman class that would routinely mock a boy like him. Danny was born with cerebral palsy and he was limited in his ability to control coordinated muscle movements, particularly walking and speaking clearly. He had a risk for seizures, and would need immediate aid if he suffered one.

Danny lived with his mother. Danny's father had left the family a few years earlier. Danny's father suffered from alcoholism and would routinely beat Danny's mother, blaming her for Danny's CP.

Danny would not let any of the above slow him down.

On the first day of a summer camp in the mountains of North Carolina, Danny's group was enjoying the camp tour, a presentation by the camp staff describing all the activities awaiting us. Sitting on benches in front of the dining hall, we were introduced to one staff member after another, all of whom would receive an immediate "Hello!" from Danny. Those well-intentioned greetings would attract smiles from the staffers, and thinly-veiled mocking from his bunkmates.

The unmistakable rumble of a motorbike could be heard from behind the dining hall. The rumble grew to a whine, and soon our boys knew they were in for a session of dirt-track motorcycle riding. You could feel the testosterone pumping! But Danny's heart sank, knowing his lack of balance would make such two-wheeling impossible.

The staffer knew ahead of time about Danny, and arranged for a surprise. If Danny could climb the path up to the dirt track, he could drive a four-wheeler with a roll cage! The track was on the plateau of a steep hill. The ascent and ride was scheduled for the third day of camp.

During free time on day two, fueled by anticipation, Danny decided to practice the walk up the hill. Danny was befriended by a few of his bunkmates by now and they, along with his camp leader, would accompany him on his practice attempt. A few girls joined the walk and this emboldened Danny more. Unfortunately, time ran out and he was unable to finish the climb. Danny asked if he could start the walk two hours early on Day 3. Danny's quickly-expanding circle of friends all agreed to walk with him.

The walk on day three resembled a small parade. The entire freshman boys' cabin decided to make the walk together, and their female counterparts joined in. Word began to spread and kids from other groups now walked along. A few thought it was a camp activity!

Danny made it to the top, and arrived at the dirt track with ten minutes to spare. The snickers of a few days earlier evolved into a roar of affection for the hero who had conquered the hill. Those cheers continued during Danny's ride and throughout the week. Their acceptance and celebration of Danny taught them more about Christ than any lesson plan ever could.

Special needs means special planning

You may get to know a kid like Danny. What particular needs any individual may have is unique to that person. Thus, the most important thing to remember is, once again, read those health forms!

In the Danny story, the unsung hero was the camp administrator who prepared in advance for Danny's arrival, making arrangements for the four-wheeler.

Sometimes parents or youth are fearful that divulging information, and only you can determine to what extent you will need such information. In the Danny story, it was likely that both camp organizers and Danny's parents were aware that there would be physical activity. Sometimes it's not clear. Consider marking on all forms something like:

"Some moderate to strenuous physical activity is common at this event. Our youth ministry team wishes to make every effort to assist all persons in their participation of this event. To help us prepare, please inform us of any physical limitations in advance."

Get to know the full spectrum of challenges he or she faces daily. Conversation with parents and caregivers will give you insight. Train and educate your leaders so they can assist while you are involved in other parts of the ministry event. Encourage mature peers of the child to befriend and assist when possible.

Types of Special needs to know about

Like Danny, many children are diagnosed at a very early age. Down syndrome and neurological ailments (like CP) are often diagnosed at birth. Other ailments like Autism Spectrum disorders are also diagnosed early in a child's life but differ in type, degree and severity. These would include Autism, which is characterized by a child's severe withdrawal from the external world, and Asperger's syndrome which is characterized by an unawareness of social cues.

All of the above can vary person to person. What is consistent with all of these special needs and many others is that they are *not* impairments to meaningful ministry experiences! You do need to plan ahead.

Pastoral Response

No one expects you to be a special care provider, a doctor or a nurse. But there are simple things you can do that will send clearly communicate to those you serve (and concerned parents): we are all created in the image and likeness of God, and everyone has an inherent human dignity which will be respected.

Some suggestions:

- **Keep a well-stocked First Aid kit.** This is less of special needs preparedness and more of "teens with any needs" items. Don't assume that dusty plastic box on the shelf has what you need for an emergency. Take it down and open it up. See what you have, and more importantly, what you need in case of an emergency. Bandages, ice packs, antiseptic ointments are standard in most kits, when they're new. But how often do you replace your first aid kid? An old kit probably needs some items replaced or recycled.

- **Is your event/meeting/Mass accessible?** The Americans with Disabilities Act requires public places to be accessible to everyone. Churches built before the ADA may have been (or need to be) refitted to accommodate people with needs. Are you traveling with a special-need student? Make sure that vehicles are safe and accessible.

- **Read your health forms!** If you haven't guessed by now, there is important information in there concerning medical needs, medications, and allergies. Any kid could have an allergic reaction to foods, pollens, insect stings, etc. Read each form.

- **Consider hiring a professional.** Kevin mentions often how he tries to have a licensed counselor and nurse on duty at all diocesan events. It's impractical to expect this for most parish activities, but it would be a special kind of stewardship for such professionals in your community to donate these services for that special weekend retreat, mission trip, etc. If attendance is not practical, have a person "on call." And if a nurse is unavailable, you may find that there are many others who are trained in first aid.

Don't go it alone. If the Holy Spirit decides to use you to bring Christ to a special-needs child with a condition you don't know about, consult a professional. There are many community advocates anxious to help you in your ministry.

Ministry with persons with special needs is challenging and requires patience and grace. But rest assured it can be some of the most rewarding ministry you'll ever lead, and some of the most rewarding peer ministry your teens will ever experience.

CHAPTER 6:

SUBSTANCE ABUSE, ADDICTION, DRUGS & ALCOHOL

"Do not conform yourselves to this age but be transformed by the renewal of your mind, that you may discern what is the will of God, what is good and pleasing and perfect...think soberly, each according to the measure of faith that God has apportioned."
(Romans 12:2-3)

Paid or unpaid, the turnover rate in youth ministry is high. It's no wonder: youth ministry is hard work! But if you fight the good fight for an extended period of time, one of the fruits of your labors is that you get to watch young people grow up before your eyes, watching our Creator transform them from awkward middle school kids to aspiring young adults chasing dreams in the real world.

In that span of six years or so the young person is forced to navigate the tumultuous waters of puberty, a time in which the child's most important organ experiences maturation: the brain.

In the first chapter we discussed the changes happening in the brain during puberty. Now we'll consider what the introduction of intoxicants does to the process.

A teen's home life plays a big role in his or her future with drugs and alcohol. Some things are beyond his or her control: a family history of abuse, dependency, or addiction increases the likelihood that the teen will also succumb to substance abuse. Some things are very much in a teenager's control. One of the most accessible places to get drugs is a parent's medicine cabinet.

Spend enough time in youth ministry and you'll read a mountain of statistics on drug and alcohol use. For every survey telling you teens are using Drug X more than ever, you can find another study that shows teens are consuming Y less. And next year the survey will be completely different. Even if we were to focus on a particular trend in drug and alcohol use, there's a likelihood that that trend could shift next year. So for the purposes of this chapter, let's simply agree on two fundamental principles:

- Drug and alcohol use—regular or experimental—leads to drug and alcohol addiction.
- There are teens in your program who use drugs and alcohol.

So it stands to reason if you minister to youth, you will encounter a teen with a substance addiction.

We have had the privilege over the years to work with the Diocese of Palm Beach's Substance Abuse Ministry Coordinator Erik Vagenius, who has been an extremely valuable resource for youth ministers in his diocese.

Vagenius points out that addiction is never lived on an island. He says that for every person struggling with substance abuse, that person will directly impact four other people, on average. In a youth ministry context that means you will not only encounter the challenge of ministering to teens and adult leaders with addictions, you'll encounter the challenge of ministering to teens that live and socialize alongside those suffering with addiction.

But rest assured, as in all other areas addressed in this book, your ministry can provide an incredible healing hand to those hurt by substance abuse and addiction.

Substance Addiction: A Spiritual Disease

Throughout the course of religion, men and women have translated religious teachings into the native tongues of those who would hear. Youth ministry uses a similar principle: translating the Gospel into "teen culture." If you wish to speak teen language, you simply cannot ignore the impact that drug and alcohol use plays on teen culture. Talk about an elephant in the room!

If we assume that teens are encountering pressure to use drugs and alcohol, we will gain credibility when we bring a much-needed Sacred Presence into this secular world.

The very simple message we wish to convey to teens is that drugs and alcohol alter who we are, and in so doing we ignore God's plan for us. Church teaching on drug use falls under the heading of respect for health and the dignity of the human person, not only to protect one's own health, but the health of others (CCC, 2284-2291).

Vagenius refers to addiction as a spiritual disease.

"Spirituality is about connectedness: with self, loved ones, and God. An addiction disconnects that person from those relationships," he said. "When we reach out and intentionally minister to the addicted person, we help reconnect people with the most important relationships in their lives, even if they don't realize it at the time."

Religion Matters

One of the most common obstacles encountered by youth ministers is the use of marijuana. It has been said that pot is the new beer, and our experience tells us that teens simply do not consider pot a serious matter.

Emphasize to your teens that the Church does not make a point in determining which drugs are more or less harmful or sinful. Any substance that is used for recreation or mind-altering is against the moral order, and that is to speak nothing about the immorality of breaking state and federal laws. The bigger question to ask is, "If it is indeed 'no big deal,' why do it?" What this dialogue usually uncovers is an overall desire to escape the dark side of a teen's life. Our job as youth ministers is to help bring light into their world. We believe strongly that a relationship with Christ can be a powerful source of strength for teens facing such pressures.

In 2001, The National Center on Addiction and Substance Abuse at Columbia University conducted a study entitled "So Help Me God: Substance Abuse, Religion and Spirituality." The results overwhelming proved that there was a connection between religion and substance abuse.

First, a pat on the back that you are already part of something that is making a difference. Quoted in that survey:

"Teens who do not believe that religious beliefs are important are almost three times likelier to drink, binge drink and smoke, almost four times likelier to use marijuana and seven times likelier to use illicit drugs than teens who strongly believe that religious beliefs are important." (10)

But for teens that are already experiencing addition, religion can be a pathway to healing. The study mentioned over and over that persons in recovery who pray or know that others are praying for them cited that prayer as a reason for their success.

Pastoral Response

As you minister to youth facing ongoing pressures to use drugs and alcohol, St. Paul reminds you that by the mercy of God, you will offer your heart and soul to these teens, and those efforts, while difficult, are holy and pleasing to God! (Romans 12:1)

Some suggestions:

- **Don't wait! Have a plan to confront it.** It is a priority to become educated about the following:

  - Is the person in front of you using or being impacted by substance abuse?
  - What is/are the substance(s)?
  - What is/are the impact(s) of this problem upon this person and/or his or her family?
  - What local resources are available in your parish/community to assist the people impacted?

  Knowing these facts help you help this person get the proper help.

  Again, it must be stressed that if you suspect that someone is at immediate risk of extreme danger, call 911.

  That being said, what you can do to help a person in the midst of these problems may include: steering them to a support group (Alcoholics Anonymous / Narcotics Anonymous, Al-Anon, Alateen, Narconon, etc.), or if your diocese is so blessed, a substance addiction ministry. Your help may be a referral to a local therapist whom you know. If you don't know any in your area, start your search with therapists who work with adolescents.

  Get to know what resources are available in your parish. Put a shout-out for caring professionals of all types in your bulletin *before* a crisis, so you know who to call before you encounter a kid with the problem. Remember, as detailed in *Renewing the Vision*, the U.S. Bishops' document on youth ministry, pastoral care strategies are both proactive and reactive. Our philosophy should generally be "do well on the former to avoid the latter."

- **Partner with parents.** We've said it before, and we'll say again here: today's generation of parents are more involved in their teens' lives. Consider having a parent track on teen drug and alcohol use, either separate or connected, so families can be educated and have an open forum to ask questions and share insights.

At the end of parent/teen discussion night on this topic, present this eye-opener: "Raise your hand if you know where to get drugs at your school." You and the parents may be shocked to find how many hands go up. Drug users are where drugs are. That can be school, church (Jim was offered drugs for the first time at a parish youth event, at the age of 10), or right down the hall at home.

Vagenius strongly recommends middle school as the ideal age to start drug and alcohol education programs.

- **Outsource.** We cannot stress enough that youth ministries should make every effort to dedicate one program a year to the topic of substance abuse and addiction. This is often neglected because on the surface it's a secular matter, and we have plenty of church-related themes already on the to-do list.

  Do not feel that you have to be an expert on the topic. Outsource! We have had the fortune of utilizing the diocesan-sponsored Substance Abuse Ministry in the Diocese of Palm Beach under the direction of Vagenius. He relishes the opportunity to speak to youth programs and schools. Many social service agencies exist for the sole purpose of reaching out to ministries like yours. Oftentimes the presentations are funded by grants, so they're absolutely free. Courts often sentence young men and women who have committed drug and alcohol-related crimes to community service that might include speaking to youth. Start with a call to your local United Way, Crisis Hotline, or Juvenile Detention Center. The operators can usually point you in the right direction.

- **Substance abuse and the power of prayer.** Whether it's in your Prayers of the Faithful in Mass or an impromptu pass-the-candle prayer, pray for young people suffering from addiction and for young people facing pressure to use drugs and alcohol. There are likely teens in your program who have an "it's no big deal" attitude, and may be surprised to hear that prayer. It will likely hit close to home for more than a few people present, and is a subtle yet effective way to bring sacredness to this secular issue.

As you continue to offer a youth ministry program that is an alternative to the things that "conform to this age," (Romans 12:2), remember that recovery is slow, hard work that most often includes setbacks. The topic is emotionally charged, and all involved will be wrestling with ugly facts about themselves and/or loved ones. Do not forget: God leads with mercy.

Life Teen Resources
The following Life Nights address the topics of alcohol, drugs and addiction within a youth group setting:
- Under the Influence
- Secret Ingredient

All Life Teen resources can be downloaded by subscribing parishes at www.catholicyouthministry.com

Chapter 7:

WHEN STORMS COME: DEALING WITH SUDDEN TRAGEDY

"You drew me forth from the womb, made me safe at my mother's breast. Upon you I was thrust from the womb; since birth you are my God. Do not stay far from me, for trouble is near, and there is no one to help."
(Psalm 22:10-12)

In 2005, we were privileged to lead a session for adult youth leaders at the National Catholic Youth Conference in Atlanta. We facilitated a discussion on how to provide a ministry response to tragedy. It was a few months after Hurricane Katrina ravaged the Gulf Coast during a late summer and fall that saw multiple storms impact lives throughout the southeast. Jim boarded a plane for NCYC just days after Hurricane Wilma caused damage to his south Florida home.

We were prepared to facilitate a dialogue with youth ministers about the hurricanes, and how they were handling the despair of the teens and families they serve.

A substantial number of those youth ministers did show up, and so did youth ministers from Seattle to New England, Arizona to Maine, *hundreds* of youth ministers wanting to know what to do when:

1. There is a sudden death in the Youth Ministry community, either directly or family
2. There is a local tragedy
3. There is a local natural disaster
4. There is a scandal within the local church

5. Other. Insert challenging situation here: _____

We found that most were youth leaders who faced death (suicides, car accidents, etc.), addiction, and more. We could have stayed in that room the entire weekend listening to youth leaders share their stories of how their parish has—or hasn't—responded when faced with crisis.

It was then that we realized that every youth minister has a story about when they had to provide pastoral care to a hurting teen. Crisis can cause great strain to any parish or community. If you work in ministry for any length of time it is very likely that you will have to work through some of them.

The difference between dealing with crisis and dealing with the other kinds of "elephants" in the room previously discussed is that these elephants are not silent. They stampede into your room, knocking down walls and trumpeting loudly.

You will be called on to serve, perhaps in the midst of your own personal grief.

Ministry of Presence

The most important skill to remember in the midst of tragedy is very simple: *presence*. In times of tragedy you may feel unqualified to deal with some of the emotional issues and physical needs of your group member(s), and you should always seek qualified helpers; but remember in the midst of tragedy your *availability* will be as important as your ability. Be present with those who need aid or comfort. Sometimes just having a place for people to gather can begin the grief process.

It is at these times when we have to turn off that youth minister instinct to create a good program! When you gather together to grieve, there should be very little "programming" going on, but they can be unforgettable youth ministry experiences. There will be more questions than answers, there will be tears and laughter, hugs and anger, and real, raw human emotion and behavior.

Whereas St. Anselm wrote that our inclination to religion is "faith seeking understanding," in tragedy it is perhaps more accurate to describe our instinct to be "faith seeking comfort."

Open your parish hall to gather together, reflect, pray, and grieve. You will likely find your building filled with teens, and don't be surprised if many of them are teens you wouldn't see at your regular youth programs.

Another kind of youth ministry "elephant" is revealed in the midst of crisis: Catholic youth that are registered to a parish but would never participate in your ongoing calendar of activities. We know there are teenage "Chreaster" Catholics, too, the ones we hoped to see after Confirmation but realistically knew they probably wouldn't be leading a Scripture study anytime soon. But when tragedy strikes, if you have done your due diligence in continuously reaching out and inviting them and seeing them in the community, you *will* see these students. Youth ministry is much larger than any youth group.

You've heard youth ministry experts say over and over again that relational ministry is the key to effective youth ministry programming: go to football games, go to plays, be a chaperone for proms, be seen in the community. While those things are always important, the time you spend in relational ministry will establish trust for when they need you the most.

If the youth you serve make it through four years of high school without a car accident, an overdose, a shooting, a natural disaster or a suicide, hit your knees and thank God. It's best, however, to assume one or more of these things *will* happen, and to be prepared when they do.

So before you even begin to strategize about how to respond when a crisis hits your town, remember that being there is half the battle. Now for the other half!

What's the plan, Stan?

Most school systems have an emergency management plan for when tragedy strikes. What is yours? Meet with local school officials to gather ideas, and, if you are the youth ministry coordinator, to make sure you are included on their emergency contact list.

If you assume that tragedies will strike at some point, it stands to reason that you should have a list of community resources and phone numbers on hand. We have developed a *Pastoral Care Resource List*, which is a good template to use for planning ahead. This can be found on page 83.

Smart people don't need to know all the answers, they need to know where to find them. There are great people in your community and beyond ready to help. Network with them. You hope you never need that list, but assume you will.

Stress

Understand that the behavior of already-stressed teens will be greatly impacted when the additional burdens of a tragedy-induced stress are also placed onto their shoulders. The teen's pre-crisis health will determine how he or she handles stress during and after a crisis.

Remember also to take into account what impact the crisis is having on *you*. We must at times keep our professional distance in times of emergency. None of us—young or old—goes through these events unchanged. It is perfectly normal and healthy to acknowledge your own grief, sadness, and frustration to those who walk along you on your ministry journey. But keep in mind that youth ministry is not meant to be therapy for you. Have a support group outside of youth ministry.

presence & Presence

It is important for the young people in your group to see you depend on Jesus Christ for healing and support. So offer a ministry response that not only gives teens presence, but also His Presence. Ours is a faith that believes in God Who transcends our human understanding of time and space and is fully alive and fully present here and now! We can touch and feel our Trinitarian God, and in the midst of crisis, how cathartic that we can confront our Creator in a very real way.

Present the true presence of God to your young people: that our Incarnate God is here in Spirit, Word, and Eucharist, with the explanation that God does not cause bad things to happen, but knows well our joy and suffering, and seeks a relationship with us in all times, good and bad.

This is not to say that the morning of a tragedy our first impulse should be to bring everyone into a beautiful, well-crafted Adoration service. (Let that be part of your long-term plan!) In the first few days after a crisis you will have a wide rage of emotions. Some grow closer to God in the midst of tragedy, others express anger. Model this for the young people, and encourage them to bring all of their emotions to Christ.

> *"Come to me, all you who labor and are burdened, and I will give you rest. Take my yoke upon you and learn from me, for I am meek and humble of heart; and you will find rest for your selves. For my yoke is easy, and my burden light." (Matthew 11:28-30)*

The *problem of evil* has plagued theologians for centuries, and you are certainly not going to stumble upon any magical insights in the midst of your crisis that explains why bad things happen to good people. Our advice for how to best handle this inevitable question: let Father do it. When you do two or three funerals a week you are bound to have addressed the problem of evil a few bazillion times. Let them cry first, and in due time, invite Father in for a Q&A.

A time to heal, and a time to catechize...

We cannot stress this enough: patience! When a crisis strikes, we know that Christ heals, and we know the awesome power of God, and the incredible power of Eucharist, and why Job would understand exactly what Billy is feeling right now, and what the Church teaches about salvation. We cannot wait to do what God put us on this earth to do: hug a teen and save a soul!

Woah! Slow down, mighty youth minister!

Your pastoral response to crisis should be both short and long term, and at least immediately you should leave your oils and catechism back at the office. A suffering teen needs to see the Incarnate Christ in you first, and that face of Christ simply needs to ask "How are you?" and mean it.

In time the crisis will give you ample opportunity to draw the young people into a holistic Catholic formation experience through both Word and Sacrament. But you won't get there until you've gone through a few boxes of tissues first.

That said, even in the initial stages of grief, even if you do nothing else but open your parish hall to crying teens, open and close with prayer. If the setting warrants it, gather before the Blessed Sacrament.

In time, infuse more theology, more intentional formation experiences, more Sacramental encounters. Offer Masses. Use your faith to seek comfort and make sense of it all. But our hunch is that if you try to do this too soon, nothing will make sense. To them or you.

When youth ministry is so much more than pizza and volleyball...

Kevin worked with a parish that recently lost a 20-something youth ministry leader and Confirmation catechist in a car accident.

He watched as the pastor opened the doors of his parish to the teens and adult leaders of the program. They gathered the day after the accident to simply pray and grieve. The teens came. They lit candles and told stories. They laughed and they cried. They asked hard questions, and Father reminded them that God's ways are not ours. The youth minister successfully managed to be a source of strength, all the while carrying her own weakness and sorrow. Another youth ministry volunteer, a close friend of the young man who had just been tragically killed, held back her own tears as she worked the phone to inform friends and loved ones near and far of what had happened.

Sometimes providing pastoral care is stepping up and providing crisis intervention, addiction prevention or response, or referral to trained professionals. Sometimes it's simply unlocking the door and letting teens gather together to cry.

Something else happened that reminds us about the power of youth ministry. The teens gathered in the worship space to pray and tell stories about the young man. But their parents came, too. So did parishioners that had little or no connection with the youth program. One by one, they, too, lit candles and said, "We didn't know him, but we are so thankful he was such a positive presence in the lives of these young people."

This is a good opportunity to remind ourselves that youth ministry is not about programs or activities, it is about relationships. The gathered programs and activities we offer are the result of relationships, and those activities help us foster relationships. Our success in ministry cannot be judged by the programs themselves.

When tragedy strikes, may your youth room truly be an Upper Room.

Pastoral Response

No one ever expects a crisis, but when it happens you will be prepared because you knew it wasn't a matter of if but when. That's not pessimism, it's professionalism. In the midst of the storm, the young people you serve will look to you for guidance, and you will be like Christ bringing great calm and quieting the storm (Matthew 8:26, Mark 4:39).

Some suggestions:

- **Prepare for the worst.** Have an emergency management plan. Be part of the emergency management plan of local schools. (Refer to *Pastoral Care Resource List* on page 83)

- **Communication is everything.** It is increasingly difficult to keep accurate records with so many different forms of communications, but when tragedy strikes, you are at the mercy of those records. Make it someone's regular task to update contact information regularly. Use multiple layers of communication; but be sure to clear what is being shared with the family or pastor first.

- **Seek out a licensed counselor, and have him or her on "retainer."** This is the same recommendation we made earlier in the depression/suicide chapter, and it bears repeating here, too. You may find there is a parishioner in your community with qualifications. In the spirit of true stewardship, ask him or her to consider sharing those talents with your ministry for free or at a significantly reduced cost.

- **Be ecumenical.** In many crisis situations, yours won't be the only faith community impacted in the community. Collaborate with youth leaders from other nearby churches to hold prayer services.

- **Network.** National youth-serving agencies have written a number of excellent resources, including lesson plans and prayer services, as a response to a variety of tragedies from school shootings to natural disasters. Consult a representative from Life Teen, the National Federation of Catholic Youth Ministry, or the many excellent publishers about what resources are available to you.

- **Remember anniversaries**. Mark down dates in your calendars, because anniversaries matter. If a teen loses a loved one, in a year most everyone will have moved on, but that teen knows the anniversary, and it will mean everything when you send the teen and his or her family a note or a card reminding them you haven't forgotten either and that you are praying for them.

Life Teen Resources
The following Life Nights can be used in times of tragedy within a youth group setting:
- Hope
- Nailed

All Life Teen resources can be downloaded by subscribing parishes at www.catholicyouthministry.com

Chapter 8:

WHEN THE ELEPHANT IS YOU

"Whoever wishes to come after me must deny himself, take up his cross, and follow me. For whoever wishes to save his life will lose it, but whoever loses his life for my sake will find it." (Matthew 16:24-25)

Employment Opening: Searching for spiritually-alive, serious-minded, fun-loving, yet theologically-proficient adult to work strange hours for laughable pay. Your responsibilities include, but are not limited to: the lives, souls, behaviors and misbehaviors of every young person within and beyond the parish. Intentional catechesis to, Christian leadership skills development of, and responsible relational ministry for the previously mentioned lives and souls and their immediate friends and families. You will get dirty, wet, and even soaked. Experience with all manners of technology and first aid preferred. Changes of job description are at the whim of the Pastor, Diocese, Youth Leadership Team, concerned parents, anonymous parishioners with strong opinions, or anyone else. Hours: all of them. Must like pizza. Applicants should submit letter of interest, resume, certificate of safe environment compliance and at least one really cool t-shirt design to Youth Ministry Search Committee ASAP.

Truly by the grace of God great people all around the world answer this job description often, and as impossible a task it may seem, we get up each morning (eventually), grab a stiff cup of coffee, pass by the secretary ("I wish *I* could just stroll in that late"), and go to work for the best CEO there is.

Whenever we meet youth ministers (paid coordinators, team members, or any level of volunteer servants) we are amazed by the efforts and sacrifices you make for Christ's young Church. God bless you. You do valuable and important work that truly affects eternity! By now you have learned that there is very little affirmation in church work. So, whether we've ever met, ever will meet or not, from two co-workers in the vineyard to another please allow us to reach up from this page and give you an overdue pat on the back.

We also hear many tales of long hours, stressed families, struggles of finances and time management, poor diet and exercise habits, and other factors that can lead to chronic exhaustion or "burnout."

There was a speaker at a youth ministry conference who once said something about the average turnover rate of youth ministers was something like two or three years. I'm pretty sure he's out of the business now.

Forget the usual suspects—the hours, the difficult teen issues, the low pay—we believe the biggest reason why youth ministers burn out is because the work is never done.

In the business world, success is measured in hard numbers. Garbage in, garbage out, if you will. But in ministry, even if we were paid handsomely, even if we were given a huge staff and a huge budget, access to a company van, an expense account and a personal chef, on your best day at the end of that day you would know there was a teen that has not yet met Christ.

The synoptic Parable of the Sower (Mark 4:3-9, Matthew 13:3-9, Luke 8:5-8) is a powerful story for youth ministers. Sometimes you will see the fruit of your labor a hundredfold: those moments when a teen tells you what an impact the ministry has had on him or her, or when the mocking teens cheer on the special-needs student, or a former troubled teen comes back a few years later to join the youth ministry team as a young adult.

But more often you will lie in bed wondering if the ministry you lead is really making a difference. Sometimes the seeds you plant will fall on rocky soil, and it may be years before the winds of the Spirit blow them back onto fertile ground. Even more frustrating is when you plant a seed that you know has the capability of producing an orchard of fruit, only to see it wither or choked by thorns.

We should always remember that our job is to plant seeds, not grow fruit. We also have to come to grips with the realization that our success is not measured by quarterly earnings figures, but in God's time, across Salvation History.

You may be familiar with the popular Old Testament passage from Ecclesiastes, about seasons:

"There is an appointed time for everything, and a time for every affair under the heavens." (3:1)

The passage goes on to speak about a time to be born, and a time to die, a time to plant, and a time to reap, and well, by now you're already singing that old Byrds song in your head. Well, at least some of you are. If you're not, seriously young whippersnapper, you have a gazillion MP3's in your iPod but don't have that classic? C'mon.

Back to the point. Qoheleth, the Hebrew translation of the name of the book's author, continues to write about the need to seek balance in all of our duties, or seasons. What isn't included in the Byrd's song is a line shortly after his list of contrasting seasons:

"He has made everything appropriate to its time, and has put the timeless into their hearts, without men's ever discovering, from beginning to end, the work which God has done." (3:11)

We must take comfort in that! Someday, somehow, God will make known the fruits of our labor.

But for now, we're left overworked, stressed out, and in need of something stronger than coffee to help us build the Kingdom. And it seems like we're always in the season of planting, never able to reap.

We live our lives and serve the Lord. We do our best to maintain balance, but the balance can be easily tipped by illness, job stress or loss, family emergencies, changes in parish leadership, vision, or direction. The list goes on, but the point is clear: before we provide "a compassionate presence in imitation of Jesus' care of people, especially those who were hurting and in need," (*Renewing the Vision*, The Ministry of Pastoral Care) we need to take care of ourselves for whatever time and season.

Areas of self-maintenance

Physical Health: What do you eat? The "youth ministry diet" of pizza, junk food and sugary soft drinks is unhealthy if followed all week long, and can be a precursor to Type II Diabetes. Based on your hours, eating out may be your only option, and based on your budget, fast food is virtually unavoidable. But, believe it or not, most fast food restaurants do offer healthier options.

When it comes to feeding your teens, pizza is often the easiest, most cost-effective way to feed lots of people. But if you reach out and survey your parishioners, you may find someone in the restaurant business willing to work with you and your ministry. Or establish a food ministry with parishioners whose only job is to provide tasty but healthier food for your events and gatherings. When there's better food for the teens, there's better food for you, because we know you won't pass up a free meal.

Occasional long (or sleepless) nights come with the territory in youth ministry, but a lack of sleep will negatively affect daytime functioning. Long-term sleep deprivation causes the prefrontal brain to shut down and causes over-reaction to negative experiences. An official citation for that comes from *Current Biology* in their October 23, 2007 edition, but if you've ever snapped at a loved one (or your Pastor) after a retreat, lock-in, pilgrimage or service trip, they didn't need some scientists to tell them you were a jerk. We've learned to apologize in advance. "Honey, on Sunday I may be really cranky. I'm sorry for anything I may say."

Exercise is also critical. You don't have to train for a marathon, but you do have to do something to run off the pizza and junk food. A healthy exercise regimen is also more than simply maintaining your physique. Because ministry never ends, it's very easy to spend your "free time" on Facebook checking up on those you serve, or emailing your Core Team about the next meeting, or writing an awesome prayer service that's just perfect for this Sunday, or, so on, so on. A half-hour jog, a slow-pitch softball game, or hiking with the spouse and kids will give you a season to laugh and dance.

Peer Support: With whom do you share your joys and concerns? Do you have anyone to discuss the realities of your ministry, someone who understands the uniqueness of the work, but will also keep you accountable? We all are called to live in the community Christ has given us. We *need* the larger body. A "lone wolf" mentality will exhaust even the strongest of youth ministers.

Family Support: We have seen too many families hurt or even broken by youth ministry. What we do is bear our soul in a very real and intimate way. We make ourselves vulnerable. We are, in a sense, married to our ministry. For those of you who have made a covenant with God through the Sacrament of Holy Matrimony, you must always remember your vocation is not youth ministry, it's your marriage. We too have been guilty of giving ourselves completely over to those we serve, only to have nothing left by the time we come home. If you schedule a time-consuming event, make sure you schedule a date night a few days later.

For those with kids, youth ministry can be a blessing and a curse. The kids love when you take them on amusement park trips, and they love when you bring home leftover pizza. But they also will miss you one or more nights a week. More importantly, they will see you enter into meaningful, intimate relationships with other children. Give yourself a thorough self-examination on this one, and leave no doubt in your kids' minds about who comes first.

The best advice we have is to make every effort to make your family a part of your ministry. Not only will it help them to understand what you're doing when you're gone, it will remind the teens that your family is the most important thing in your world, and will reinforce the notion that ministry isn't our primary vocation.

As for extended family, well, do your best. We are married to the best two women on the planet, and we're both fairly certain neither of our fathers-in-law ever dreamed of someday walking down the aisle and handing their daughters over to youth ministers. Your own parents may not ever quite realize what it is you do for a living. Be proud and convicted of who you are and what you do, and don't be afraid to actually tell them what you do for a living. Share the passion. They still might not understand what you do, but they won't doubt for a second your dedication.

Spiritual Growth: Is your ministry your faith experience? DANGER! We need to continue to seek our time alone with our Lord. We need to take time to worship, to spend time in prayer, communally and individually, and to break open scripture. Jesus promises us if we seek him he will nourish us:

"I am the bread of life; whoever comes to me will never hunger, and whoever believes in me will never thirst." (John 6:35)

Have you ever said this? "I'm sorry God, I don't have time for you today! I'm too busy doing youth ministry!"

Before you search for a wifi signal to check Facebook first thing Monday morning, make it a priority to schedule time during the work week to reflect alone with Christ, asking for clarity, patience, strength, wisdom, and the ability to yield to God's Will.

Also, if possible, plan to take an annual retreat, or at least enroll in some kind of spiritual program. Just make sure you are not in charge!

We also recommend having a spiritual advisor and a confessor. Consider having these roles filled by persons who have no vested interest in your youth ministry program, as they can provide unique perspectives on your ministry, your ministry leadership, and the spirituality you bring to them.

Finally, we would be remiss if we didn't encourage you to seek help when you need it. The caregiver needs care, too. Make sure you are whole before you try to provide care to the broken. If you require treatment or counseling or Reconciliation, get it.

We don't know who first said it, but it bears repeating. When it comes to youth ministry, or any lay ecclesial ministry for that matter, the pay is lousy, but the benefits are out of this world.

May you continue to worship and serve the Lord with gladness. (Psalm 100:2)

PASTORAL CARE RESOURCE LIST

National Phone Numbers

AIDS
- CDC AIDS Information (800) 232-4636

ALCOHOL/DRUGS
- Nat. Council on Alcoholism and Drug Dependence Hopeline (800) 622-2255
- Nat. Help Line for Substance Abuse (800) 262-2463

CHILD ABUSE
- Child Help USA National Child Abuse Hotline (800) 422-4453
- Covenant House (800) 999-9999

CRISIS & SUICIDE
- Girls & Boys Town National Hotline(800) 448-3000
- Nat. Suicide Prevention Lifeline (800) 273-TALK

DOMESTIC VIOLENCE
- Nat. Domestic Violence Hotline (800) 799-SAFE
- Nat. US Child Abuse Hotline (800) 4-A-CHILD

MEDICAL
- American Assoc. of Poison Control Centers (800) 222-1222

OTHER
- Eating Disorders Awareness & Prevention (800) 931-2237
- CyberTipline (Internet exploitation & abuse)
  (800) 843-5678

RAPE AND SEXUAL ASSAULT
- Rape, Abuse, and Incest National Network (RAINN)
  (800) 656-HOPE
- Nat. Domestic Violence/Child Abuse/ Sexual Abuse
  (800) 799-7233
- Abuse Victim Hotline (866) 662-4535

RUNAWAY
- Nat. Runaway Switchboard (800) RUNAWAY
- Nat. Hotline for Missing & Exploited Children (800) THE-LOST

Local Number/Contact

LOCAL COMMUNITY HELPLINE(S):

_____

_____

_____

_____

DIOCESAN OFFICE(S)
- Diocesan Director of Youth Ministry:

_____

- Diocesan Safe Environment Office*:

_____

*YM Coord. should know the diocesan Safe Environment Policy

LIST OF AGENCIES FOR REPORT OF SEXUAL OR PHYSICAL ABUSE OR NEGLECT*

- City/County Agency:

_____

_____

_____

- State Agency:

_____

_____

_____

*YM Coord. should know the reporting laws for your state and/or municipality

COUNSELING
- Licensed Mental Health Counselor(s):

_____

_____

_____

_____

_____

_____

SCHOOLS*
- Principal's Office and/or Campus Minister numbers for all high schools in your area:

_____

_____

_____

_____

_____

_____

_____

_____

_____

* It's a good idea to have a basic knowledge of these schools' emergency action plans. Know how you'll fit in.

OTHER
- If possible, ask your parish's office manager for an updated database of all registered teens in your parish (including teens that generally do not participate in youth ministry activities). When tragedy strikes, it will come in handy.

- Emergency/Cellular phone numbers of Adult Leadership Team & Pastor & Priests. If tragedy strikes, notify your parish priests ASAP.

_____

_____

_____

This resource was developed for youth ministry leaders by Jim Chesnes & Kevin Driscoll. Adapt as needed for your pastoral situation. National numbers are courtesy of PsychCentral.com and should be checked periodically for accuracy.